First published in Great Britain in 2000 by
David & Charles Children's Books,
Winchester House, 259-269 Old Marylebone Road, London NW1 5XJ

Text © Adèle Geras 2000
Illustrations © Emma Chichester Clark 2000

The rights of Adèle Geras and Emma Chichester Clark to be identified as the author
and illustrator of this work have been asserted by them in accordance with the
Copyright, Designs and Patents Act, 1988.

ISBN: 1 86233 246 0

A CIP catalogue record for this title is available from the British Library.

Printed and bound in Belgium

The Magic of the Ballet

Sleeping Beauty

RETOLD BY ADÈLE GERAS
ILLUSTRATED BY EMMA CHICHESTER CLARK

David & Charles
Children's Books

The Magic of the Ballet

HUMAN BEINGS LIKE TO move their bodies in time to rhythm. Even the tiniest babies enjoy being rocked or gently bounced as you sing to them, and we all know how feet long to move when we hear a strong and exciting beat. "That's toe-tapping music," we say, and what we mean is we would like to dance to it.

There are many different kinds of dance: folk, disco, ballroom, tap and so on.

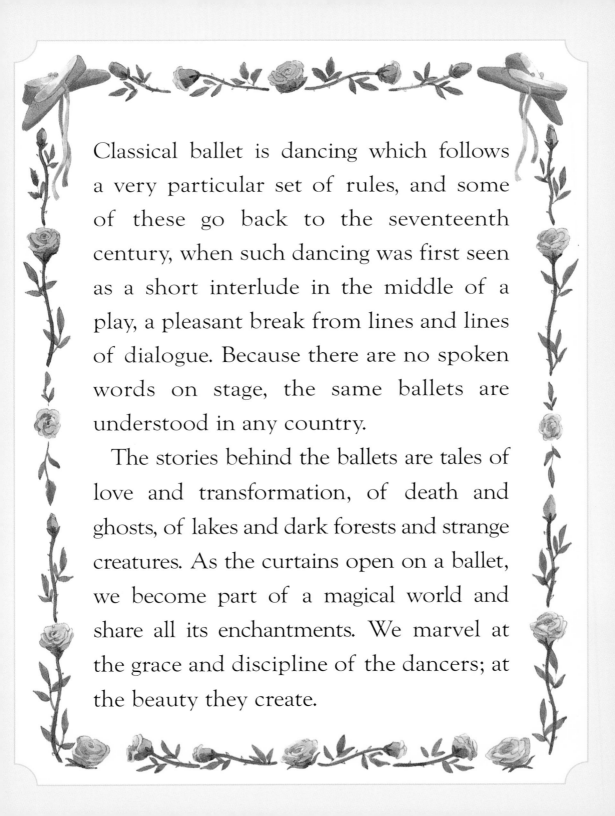

Classical ballet is dancing which follows a very particular set of rules, and some of these go back to the seventeenth century, when such dancing was first seen as a short interlude in the middle of a play, a pleasant break from lines and lines of dialogue. Because there are no spoken words on stage, the same ballets are understood in any country.

The stories behind the ballets are tales of love and transformation, of death and ghosts, of lakes and dark forests and strange creatures. As the curtains open on a ballet, we become part of a magical world and share all its enchantments. We marvel at the grace and discipline of the dancers; at the beauty they create.

'Tiny droplets of blood had stained her dress.'

Sleeping Beauty

MY NAME IS CARABOSSE. People call me all sorts of things. The Bad Fairy, the Wicked Fairy, or the Black Fairy are the most common, but Carabosse is what I prefer. I am old. I am the oldest fairy in the kingdom, and for this reason, if for no other, you would think that King Florestan and his wife would have seen to it that I received an invitation for what promised to be quite the most glittering event in the social calendar: the christening of their longed-for baby daughter, Aurora. They thought (and this is their excuse and it is too feeble to be anything but an excuse) that I had retired. Invitation or not, I went anyway.

"No one had seen you," King Florestan told me at the party, "for ages and ages, and we all thought you had retired, or emigrated."

"Quite the reverse," I said. I was enjoying his embarrassment. In fact, once I had made my entrance, I was determined to enjoy the whole party as much as possible. The best thing of all was the surprise and dismay I caused as I arrived at the door. No one was expecting me.

The entire palace staff had been running about for hours, laying on enough food to feed an army, polishing the wooden floors, dusting down the chandeliers, and wreathing marble columns with garlands of roses. I had seen them in my magic mirror. I'd been watching them for days, and they'd known nothing about it.

At first I thought that I would leave them to get on with the celebrations, but when I saw them gathering near the cradle, oohing and aahing and behaving in a thoroughly silly fashion, I decided to punish them. I was in a very bad temper that day, I admit. I decided, in the blink of an eye, that Princess Aurora would have to perish. That would wipe the smile off their faces, oh yes indeed! What a lesson it would be for King Florestan and the Queen! How dare they invite the others and leave me out?

By the time I reached the palace, (having tossed a few thunderbolts and lightning flashes out of the coach as I passed over the garden, just to announce myself) the other fairies had already given Princess Aurora their gifts. These were exactly the sort of thing I had come to expect from my predictable relations: Joy, Beauty, Intelligence and so forth. Naturally, all the present-giving stopped as soon as I stepped into the room. That was when poor Florestan started mumbling his excuses, but I wasn't interested in listening to him. I went straight to the cradle and said, "I have a gift for the Princess Aurora. Sixteen years of happiness and beauty. And after that, I'm afraid, she will

prick her finger on a spindle and drop down dead."

Then I flung myself into my black coach.

"Fly!" I said to the moths that pulled it along. "Fly away. We are not wanted here."

I did feel a great deal better after that, but not for long. When I looked into my magic mirror to see what the effect of my announcement was, I discovered that the Lilac Fairy had not yet bestowed her gift. There she was, right before my eyes, busy undoing some of my magic. How dare she!

"Princess Aurora will not die," she was saying, "but sleep for a hundred years until she is woken by a prince's kiss."

I was angrier than ever. What good to me was a hundred-year sleep? Kisses from a handsome prince were no part of my plan. I was seething with rage. I went to bed that night vowing to outwit the Lilac Fairy even if it took me sixteen years to do it. How dare she pit her puny powers against me, the wicked fairy Carabosse? I became more determined than ever that the Princess Aurora would not have her life for very long. I would attend to it, even if it were the last thing I ever did.

I, the Lilac Fairy, don't like to speak unkindly of anyone, but I make an exception when it comes to Carabosse. She is so wicked, evil and ugly that whatever one says about her can never be too harsh.

Still, the way Carabosse behaved at poor Princess Aurora's christening shocked us all. It was the purest good luck that I had not yet given the baby my gift and so I was able to soften the ill-wishing just a little.

It's done now. Sixteen years we have waited and now the waiting is over. Princess Aurora

is asleep in her chamber, with King Florestan and his Queen on comfortable chairs nearby. I have enchanted everyone, and every living thing from the footmen, fast asleep in the corridor, to the cat curled up by the cold fireside. They will not wake for one hundred years. It is very quiet in the palace now. There

will be only dust, gathering on the surfaces of things, because the spiders are asleep and can spin no webs at all. I shall raise a forest of thorns and brambles around the building to shield it from sight until the right person comes to break the spell. It is strange to remember that until a few hours ago we had begun to believe that all would be well.

King Florestan banned spindles from his kingdom within minutes of Carabosse's pronouncement. The very next day, there was a bonfire in the market square, and people came from the furthest corners of the

land to throw their spindles into the flames. How the fire leapt and roared and how we rejoiced to see that everything that could possibly threaten Princess Aurora was being reduced to ashes.

Then the years slid by, faster than anyone could have imagined, and before we knew where we were, it was the Princess' sixteenth birthday. One of my sisters had bestowed on her the gift of beauty, and in her birthday dress she was as lovely as a rosebud. Every rose in the palace garden had bloomed in her honour and there were garlands everywhere. Four young princes from neighbouring territories had come to offer themselves as suitors for her hand, and although she danced with them in the most delightful way possible, I could see that she would love none of these. Do not ask me how. It is simply my duty as a fairy to know such things, just as I knew that whatever the King and Queen thought, the danger from Carabosse was still something to be reckoned with.

Still, even I, intoxicated with joy and sunshine and the fragrance of the roses, let my guard slip a little. I should have been more careful, more vigilant. I shall never cease to blame myself.

A crowd gathered to wish the Princess well. One old lady hobbled up to her with a pretty bunch of flowers. It would have been difficult to refuse such an offering. Princess Aurora took it and thanked the old lady kindly. As the old crone shuffled slowly away into the crowd, something about her seemed to remind me of Carabosse. I would have spoken, but all eyes were on Aurora. She, it seemed, had pricked herself on a thorn. Perhaps the roses in the bouquet had not been carefully trimmed. In any case, she had fainted from the shock, and tiny droplets of blood had stained her dress.

Just then the old lady threw back her hood and cackled, "Oh, look at you all! Fools! Did you think you could defeat me? Idiots! I am Carabosse, and there, in the flowers you will find hidden a spindle. So much for your precious Princess Aurora!"

She flapped her black cloak about her and vanished in a puff of foul-smelling smoke. I took charge at once.

"Bring the Princess to her bedchamber. It has come to pass exactly as I predicted. Let everyone who does not live in the palace leave instantly. We have miracles to perform."

Everyone left the garden. Princess Aurora was carried to her bed and the rest was easy.

Now they are all sleeping. The forest of briars and thorns is growing even as I speak. Princess Aurora is safe. I, the Lilac Fairy, will guard her for the next hundred years, until the spell is broken. A hundred years is but the twinkling of an eye for me. It will pass.

❧

This has been the strangest day's hunting I've ever had. I set out to find deer and I found – well, let me tell you the story.

My name is Florimund. I am a prince of the royal blood. We, my companions and I, had decided to explore the hills and valleys beyond our own borders, and that was how we found ourselves in a forest that I had never seen before. There were no proper trees in this place, only towering brambles and thickets of wild roses. My hunting party grew nervous and begged me to turn back, but I was fascinated by this place.

"You go," I said, "and I will come after you later. I wish to find what is hidden in the heart of this prickly maze."

So they left me and the silence all around filled my ears. The daylight was fading.

You can imagine how astonished I was, then, when five beautiful ladies suddenly appeared

before me. Their leader, covered in a lilac cloak, stepped forward.

"Do not be afraid, Prince Florimund," she said as she looked into my eyes.

"How do you know my name?" I asked.

"I know very many things," she answered. "I know, for instance, who your true love will be. She is closer than you know."

I smiled at this. If she knew everything, how could she not know that I already had my eye on Valentina, the fairest maid in my kingdom?

"I am already in love," I said.

"That is what you think," whispered the lady in the lilac cloak. "But look first at Princess Aurora. Look first, and then tell me that you love another."

I peered through the trees, and there was the most beautiful lady I had ever seen. She glided between the dark branches like a ghost. I moved towards her. She said nothing, only danced with me. Her beauty bewitched me. Then, as quickly as she had appeared, she vanished into the shadows.

"That," said the lady in lilac, "was but a vision of the Princess. The real person is even lovelier. She has been asleep in a palace in the depths of this wood for a hundred years, but she is waiting for someone who loves her to wake her from her long slumber."

"How can I find her?" I cried. "Show me how to find her!"

For of course the Lilac Fairy was right and

I had lost my heart entirely.

"Cut down these thorns," she said to me, "and you will find your heart's desire."

She slipped away into the darkness, followed by her companions, and I was all alone. I unsheathed my sword and began to make my way through the tangled branches, cutting and slashing at anything that blocked my path. Thorns tore at the skin of my hands and face. Sharp twigs snatched at my garments. I do not know how long I spent in the forest, but after what seemed like hours, I caught sight of the white walls of the palace, glimmering in the moonlight.

I should have known that the Forces of Darkness would be lying in wait for me. I was attacked by huge, black moth-shapes, and bat-shapes, and a hideous crone with a stick and cloak, but I laid about me with my sword and drove them back into the shadows.

"Go," I shouted, "you are evil creatures

and I want nothing to do with you! Nothing is more powerful than my love."

After their shrieks had died away, I made my way into the echoing hall of the palace. Everywhere I looked, people were lying fast asleep, grey under a thick blanket of dust. The Princess, lying on her bed, had been protected by the gauzy bed-curtains. It seemed to me that she had closed her eyes only a moment ago. As soon as I saw her, I knew that I would never love another, and that Princess Aurora would be my bride. I bent over and kissed her. She stirred and opened her eyes. All around us, the palace slowly came to life, but I was unaware of it. I had broken the spell that had bewitched the Princess, but now I was enchanted in turn.

I said, "When I set out for the hunt this morning, I never dreamed that you were what I would find."

Princess Aurora smiled.

I am Aurora, bride of Prince Florimund, and my wedding party is over. Tomorrow we will set out for his home and I shall see my new kingdom. I shall miss my godmothers, the fairies, but I shall especially miss the Lilac Fairy. It is thanks to her that Carabosse has at last fled from this land and will worry us no longer. I am grateful to the Lilac Fairy for many things. She looked after me and kept me from the dangers that have beset me since the day I was born. I shall miss my parents and my home, but shall take with me happy memories of my wedding day ball.

"Who would you like," the Lilac Fairy asked, "to dance at your party?"

I was feeling whimsical, I suppose. I said,

"I would like Red Riding Hood and the Wolf, Puss-in-Boots and the White Cat, and of course the Bluebird of Happiness."

So my beloved Lilac Fairy worked her magic once again, and there they were, dancing and feasting with all the other guests. Tonight, when I close my eyes, I know that I will wake up in the morning and look into the face of my darling Florimund. The nightmares that filled my head for a hundred years, of black thorns and matted branches, are gone forever, and I shall have nothing but sweet dreams from now on.

THE SLEEPING BEAUTY WAS first put on in 1890. The music was by Tchaikovsky and the choreography by Marius Petipa. The fairytale is a very ancient one, but it was first written down in the eighteenth century by a Frenchman called Charles Perrault.

The choreographer of a ballet decides which steps should be danced on stage and in which order. They are responsible for the overall pattern of the ballet, and every individual step taken by each member of the cast.

There have been many famous choreographers. The work of Petipa, Nijinsky and Fokine can still be seen today, as their ideas have passed down to a new generation of choreographers who have danced the steps themselves. Modern choreographers like to add something of their own and make changes to well-known works, but one can still see ballets danced today that are very like those of a century ago.

It would be impossible to reproduce every detail of the dance from memory, and so there are two systems of notation which enable choreographers to write down sequences of steps. These have been in use since the nineteenth century. One is the method invented by Laban (Labanotation) and the other is by Benesh and is sometimes known as 'Choreology'. As dancers all over the world know the French ballet

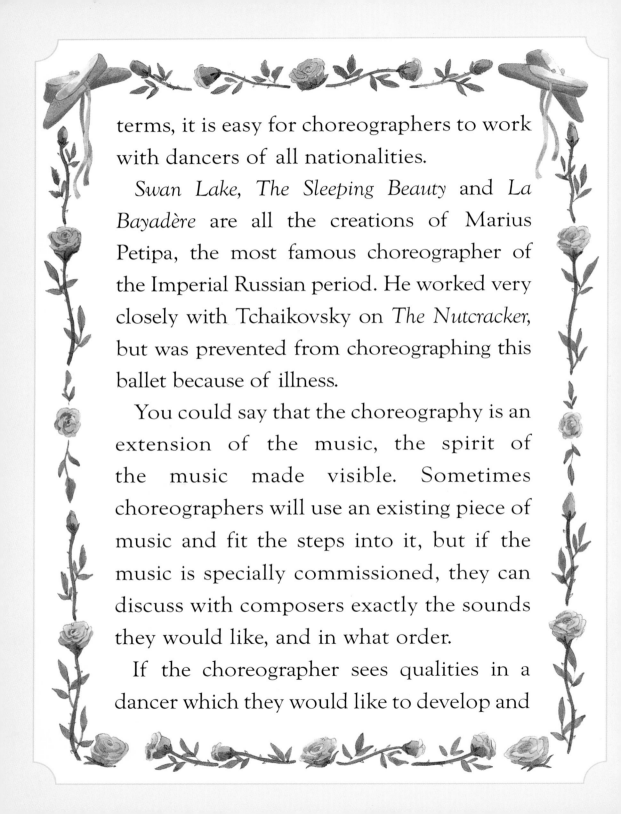

terms, it is easy for choreographers to work with dancers of all nationalities.

Swan Lake, The Sleeping Beauty and *La Bayadère* are all the creations of Marius Petipa, the most famous choreographer of the Imperial Russian period. He worked very closely with Tchaikovsky on *The Nutcracker,* but was prevented from choreographing this ballet because of illness.

You could say that the choreography is an extension of the music, the spirit of the music made visible. Sometimes choreographers will use an existing piece of music and fit the steps into it, but if the music is specially commissioned, they can discuss with composers exactly the sounds they would like, and in what order.

If the choreographer sees qualities in a dancer which they would like to develop and emphasise, they can create a whole ballet around that particular person's skills.

Choreographers have to keep in their heads not only each single dancer's movements, but the way in which a whole company of people uses the stage and fills it with constantly changing patterns. By the time we see the ballet, they are a part of the magic and seem to have grown naturally from the music.

j398.209 Geras, Adele.
/4
G   Sleeping Beauty.

$10.95

DATE			

BAKER & TAYLOR

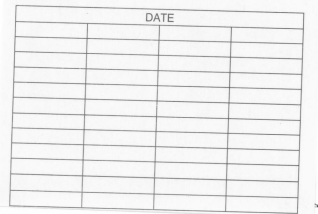